Mother and Daughter

© 2001 Havoc Publishing
San Diego, California
U.S.A.

Artwork by Annie LaPoint
Artwork © 2001 under license from Penny Lane Publishing, Inc.

Selected text by Amy Spitler
Selected text by Annie LaPoint

ISBN 0-7416-1304-2

www.havocpub.com

Made in Korea

This little book is dedicated to:

_____

From mother
to daughter
this truth must
be shared,
you are a lifetime
of gifts,
so rich
and quite rare.

A mother's

HEART

speaks

without

words.

If a mother could
read her daughter's
heart, surely she
would find-
a thankfulness for
all she's been given
and a desire to return
in kind.

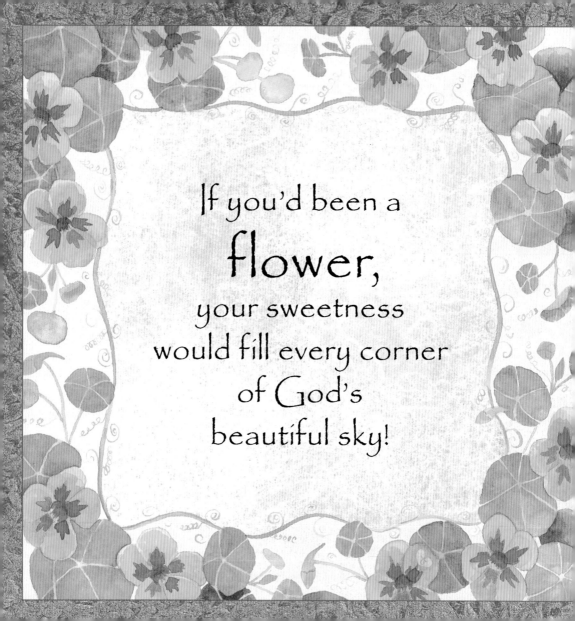

If you'd been a
flower,
your sweetness
would fill every corner
of God's
beautiful sky!

DAUGHTERS
are love
coming from a
MOTHER
vine.

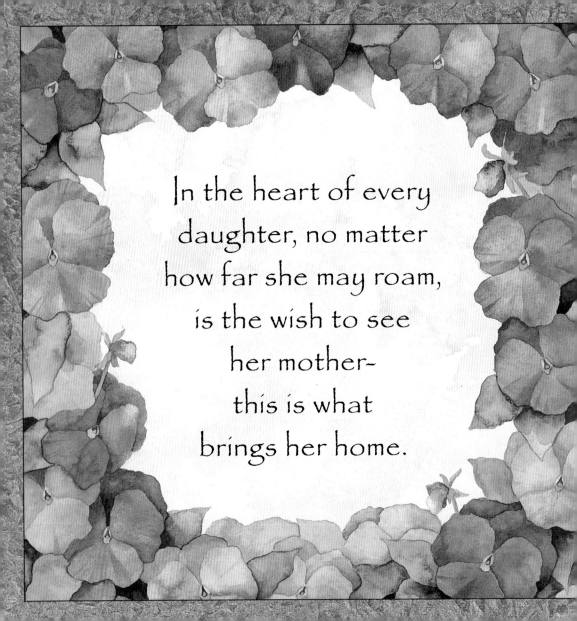

In the heart of every
daughter, no matter
how far she may roam,
is the wish to see
her mother–
this is what
brings her home.

A daughter is the

KEEPER

of her mother's

greatest

DREAMS.

Daughters

are

DELIGHTFUL!

Mothers and
Daughters
are very much alike,
each cheering the
other's victories,
and consoling in
times of strife.

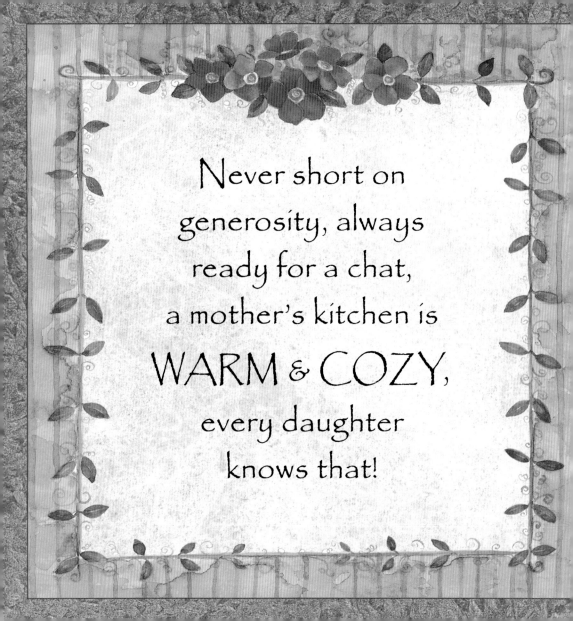

Never short on
generosity, always
ready for a chat,
a mother's kitchen is

WARM & COZY,

every daughter
knows that!

In her daughter,
a mother sees all
of her

BEST

qualities.

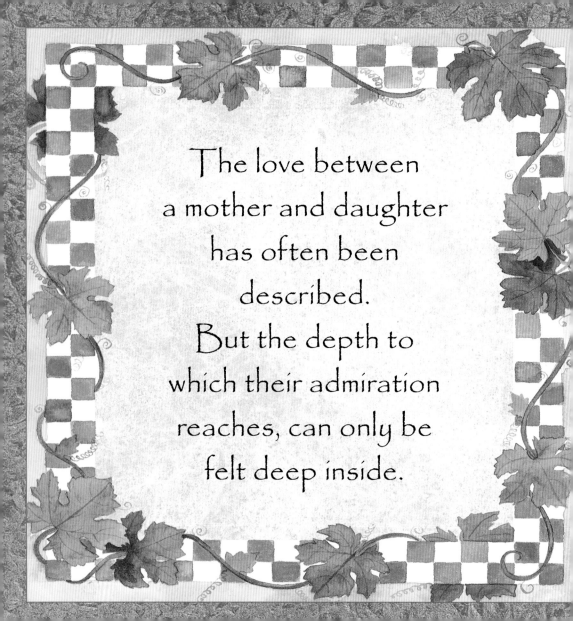

The love between
a mother and daughter
has often been
described.
But the depth to
which their admiration
reaches, can only be
felt deep inside.

Psalm 19:30

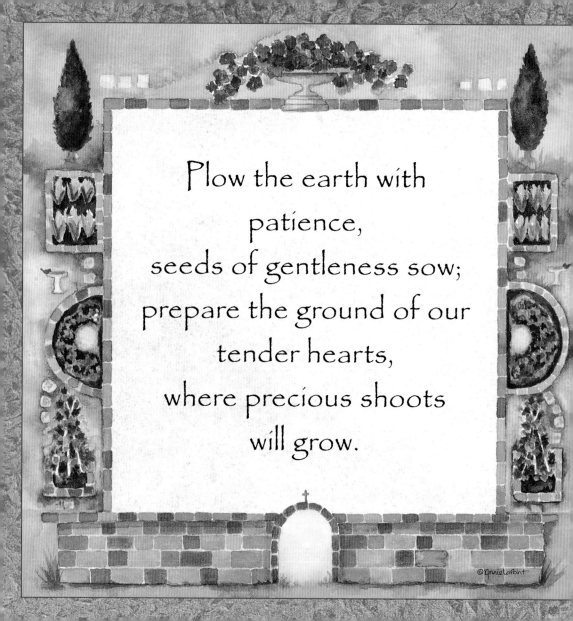

Plow the earth with
patience,
seeds of gentleness sow;
prepare the ground of our
tender hearts,
where precious shoots
will grow.

...of spring and what it will bring... al...

of spring and what it will bring... alyssum.

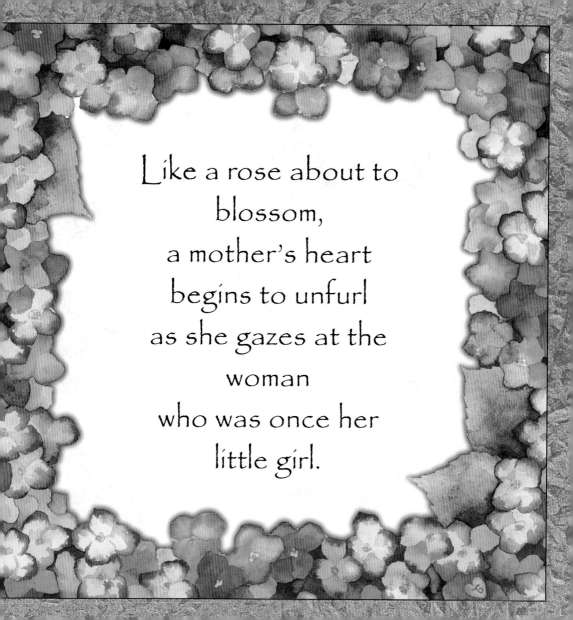

Like a rose about to
blossom,
a mother's heart
begins to unfurl
as she gazes at the
woman
who was once her
little girl.

Your mother is
your compass for life,
always pointing in the
right direction, but
leaving the steering to
YOU.

It is with her

heart

that a mother

listens.

Cultivate a heart of joy

Through my mother's
eyes,
I see others with grace;
It's through my mother's
eyes,
and the love that's
on her face.

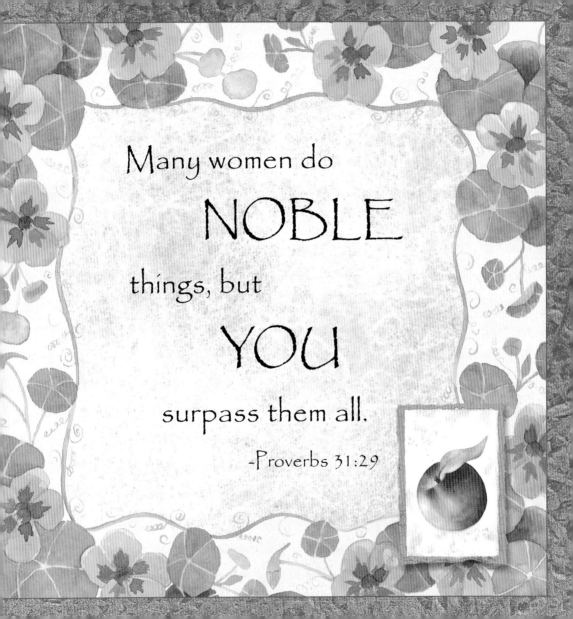

Many women do

NOBLE

things, but

YOU

surpass them all.

-Proverbs 31:29

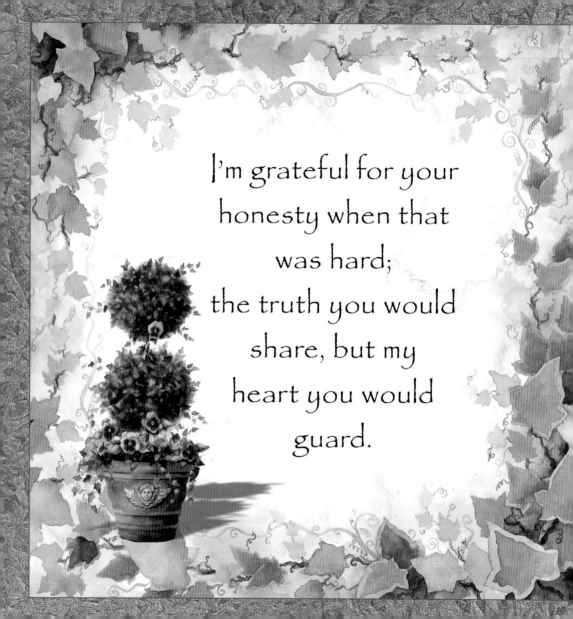

I'm grateful for your
honesty when that
was hard;
the truth you would
share, but my
heart you would
guard.

Deeper LOVE,

more than a friend,

MOTHER,

CHILD,

there is no end.

Aren't you
glad
we were
CHOSEN
for
each other?

To watch her
daughter
grow and thrive
is a mother's
greatest
pleasure...

for what her

child is to her

is a

HEAVENLY

TREASURE.

The greatest
strength a
mother
can teach her
daughter is to
TRUST
in herself.

In the
GARDEN
OF
LIFE,
a mother's love
is for all
thyme.

The landscape
of your heart is filled
with beauty,
the color of your life
is painting a
BRILLIANT
sky!

Life Begins

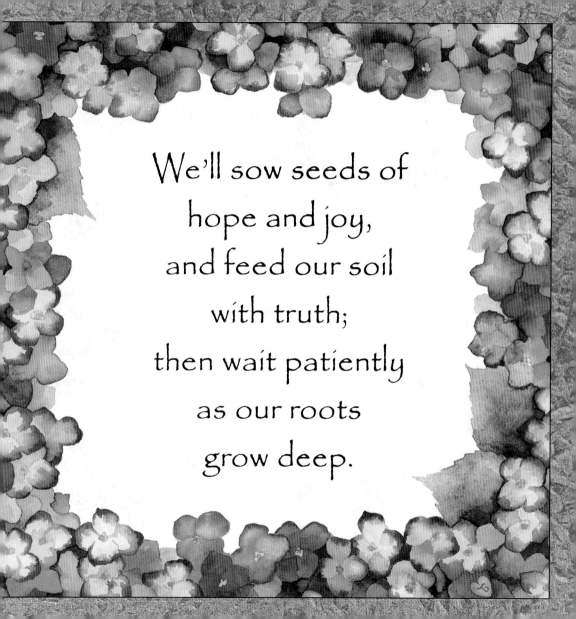

We'll sow seeds of
hope and joy,
and feed our soil
with truth;
then wait patiently
as our roots
grow deep.

Of all the lessons
learned,
the ones your
mother taught
ring
TRUEST.

A mother and a
daughter have traditions
of their own.
Unique in every way
and with appreciation
amply shown.

While roses may be
beauties with aromas
deemed divine,
a mother's love is
thornless, a GIFT
to be cherished
for all time.

The
LOVE
you invest in
your daughter
makes you a
lifelong
FRIEND.

A mother is always present in her daughter's HEART.

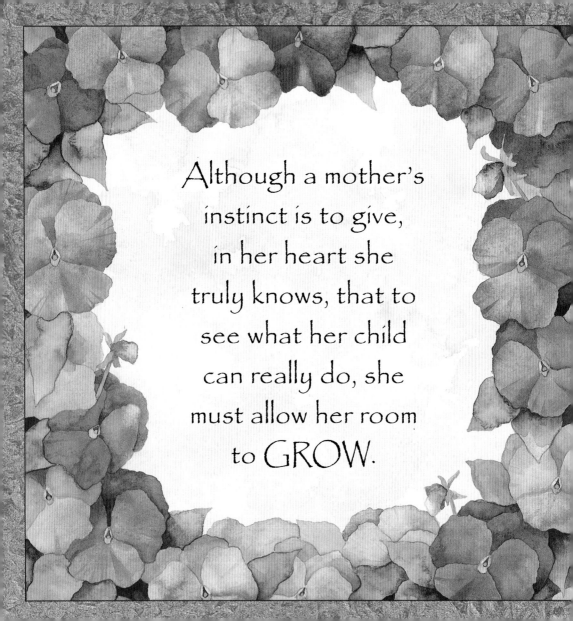

Although a mother's
instinct is to give,
in her heart she
truly knows, that to
see what her child
can really do, she
must allow her room
to GROW.

HOME
is
where
your
MOM
is.

As we stroll
down memory lane,
our past reveals
a future more clear.
Remembrances of
cherished talks as
two adults,
to each other...

we

become

more

DEAR.

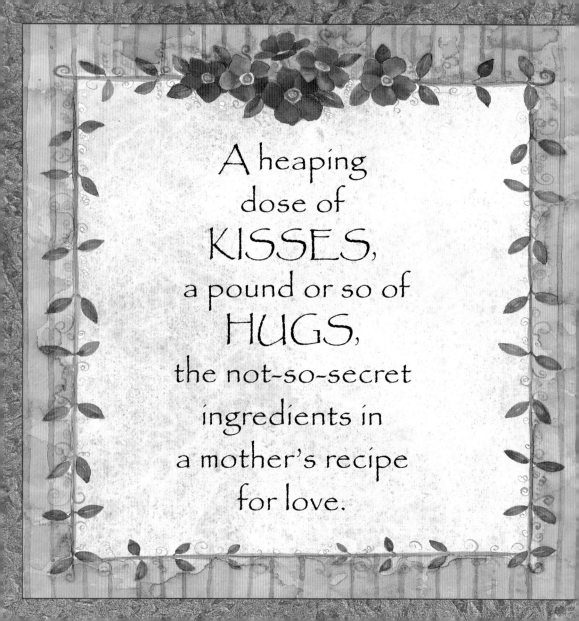

A heaping
dose of
KISSES,
a pound or so of
HUGS,
the not-so-secret

ingredients in

a mother's recipe

for love.

Every hurt
that is kissed away
in
childhood
is a daughter's
lesson
in
KINDNESS
to others.

MOTHERS
and
DAUGHTERS
are
a wonderful
story,
written
with love, laughter,
and happiness.